I0411013

July 2014

SOFTWARE LICENSES

DOD's Plan to Collect Inventory Data Meets Statutory Requirements

GAO-14-625

GAO Highlights

Highlights of GAO-14-625, a report to congressional committees

SOFTWARE LICENSES

DOD's Plan to Collect Inventory Data Meets Statutory Requirements

Why GAO Did This Study

DOD plans to spend at least $31 billion on information technology products and services in fiscal year 2014, including software licenses. Further, DOD engages in hundreds of licensing agreements annually. Effective management of software licenses can help organizations avoid purchasing too many licenses that result in unused software and/or too few licenses that result in noncompliance with license terms, which can lead to additional fees.

To help DOD effectively manage its software licenses, section 937 of the National Defense Authorization Act for Fiscal Year 2013 mandated that the department issue a plan for developing a DOD-wide inventory of selected software licenses. The accompanying Senate report mandated that GAO review the plan. In response to the Act, DOD issued the plan in July 2013.

GAO's objective was to determine whether DOD's software license inventory plan met four requirements that were specified in the act. To do so, GAO collected and analyzed key supporting materials, such as DOD's software license spend analysis, data collection instrument, and guidance provided to DOD components. GAO also interviewed officials with knowledge of the plan.

What GAO Recommends

GAO is not making recommendations. In commenting on a draft of this report, the department concurred with GAO's findings.

View GAO-14-625. For more information, contact Carol R. Cha at (202) 512-4456 or ChaC@gao.gov.

What GAO Found

The Department of Defense's (DOD) plan satisfied all four statutory requirements (see table). For example, for the first requirement, the plan contained detailed information on the scope of the inventory, including a list of over 900 software titles from publishers including Adobe, Microsoft, Oracle, and IBM; as well as a summary of the licenses not selected for inventory, such as classified software and contractor-owned software.

For the second and third requirements, the plan's software licensing data collection instrument contained key data fields necessary for the Office of the Chief Information Officer (CIO) to compare purchased licenses with installed licenses and assess the department's needs over fiscal years 2014 and 2015. While data on license count are required, data on costs are to be entered only if readily available. Office of the CIO officials told us they expect the cost data they receive will be limited, but also stated that they are investigating how these data can be stored in a more centralized and automated fashion.

Finally, for the fourth requirement, the plan outlined key analyses the DOD CIO and component CIOs expect to undertake once the department-wide inventory is complete, including assessments of license use and alternative licensing options. Among other things, these analyses could lead to savings through procuring volume discounts and/or moving toward enterprise-wide solutions; as well as disposing of excessive licenses.

Assessment of DOD's Plan for Developing an Inventory of Selected Software Licenses

Requirement	Addressed
Identify and explain the software licenses selected, and provide a summary of the software licenses not selected.	●
Provide a comparison of purchased licenses with installed licenses.	●
Describe how the department will assess its needs for selected software licenses over the 2 fiscal years following plan issuance.	●
Describe how the department can achieve the greatest economies of scale and cost savings in the procurement, use, and optimization of selected software licenses.	●

Source: GAO analysis of DOD data. | GAO-14-625

Key: ●=Addressed—DOD's plan provided evidence that addressed the requirement.

While the plan is sound, the implementation of the plan (currently under way) will be the most challenging part of this effort. The DOD CIO's ability to effectively carry out its planned cost savings analyses will largely depend on the completeness and accuracy of the information provided by the components.

Contents

Abbreviations

CIO	Chief Information Officer
DOD	Department of Defense
IT	information technology

U.S. GOVERNMENT ACCOUNTABILITY OFFICE

441 G St. N.W.
Washington, DC 20548

July 8, 2014

Congressional Committees

The Department of Defense (DOD) plans to spend at least $31 billion on information technology (IT) products and services in fiscal year 2014, including software licenses. Further, the department engages in hundreds of licensing agreements annually. Effective management of software licenses can help organizations avoid purchasing too many licenses that result in unused software and/or too few licenses that result in noncompliance with license terms, which can lead to additional fees.

To help DOD effectively manage its software licenses, section 937 of the National Defense Authorization Act for Fiscal Year 2013[1] mandated the department to issue a plan for developing a DOD-wide inventory of selected[2] software licenses. DOD issued the plan on July 18, 2013.[3] Further, the Senate report accompanying the act[4] mandated us to review and report to the congressional defense committees, on whether DOD's plan addressed the following requirements specified in the act:

1. identify and explain the software licenses selected for inventory, and provide a summary of the software licenses not selected;

2. describe how the department will compare purchased licenses with installed[5] licenses;

3. describe how the department will assess its needs for selected software licenses over the 2 fiscal years following plan issuance; and

---

[1] Pub. L. No. 112-239, § 937, 126 Stat. 1632, 1887-88 (Jan. 2, 2013). The act required DOD to issue the plan within 180 days of enactment.

[2] The act requires DOD's Chief Information Officer to select a subset of software licenses for inventory that will maximize the department's return on investment.

[3] Section 935 of the National Defense Authorization Act for Fiscal Year 2014 required DOD to update this inventory plan with additional requirements not included in the fiscal year 2013 act such as including all DOD software licenses for which a military department spends more than $5 million annually.

[4] S. Rep. No. 112-173, at 175 (2012).

[5] Installed licenses are software licenses deployed for use on a DOD-owned or controlled computer.

4. describe how the department can achieve the greatest economies of scale and cost savings in the procurement, use, and optimization of selected software licenses.

Accordingly, our objective was to determine whether DOD's software license inventory plan met statutory requirements.

On April 29, 2014, in response to our mandate, we provided congressional defense committees a briefing on the results of our study. This report summarizes the briefing and formally transmits our results to DOD. The briefing slides, which are included as appendix I of this report, also provide details on our scope and methodology.

We conducted this performance audit from March 2014 to July 2014 in accordance with generally accepted government auditing standards. Those standards require that we plan and perform the audit to obtain sufficient, appropriate evidence to provide a reasonable basis for our findings and conclusions based on our audit objectives. We believe that the evidence obtained provides a reasonable basis for our findings and conclusions based on our audit objectives.

Results in Brief

In summary, we found that DOD's plan satisfied all four statutory requirements (see table 1). For example, for the first requirement, the plan contains detailed information on the scope of the inventory, including a list of over 900 software titles from publishers including Adobe, Microsoft, Oracle, and IBM. The selected publishers were also generally consistent with those that key agencies have also told us, as part of our work on federal software licensing,[6] are being most widely used. As the act requires, the plan summarized the software licenses not selected for inventory. Specifically, it outlined that some classified software, contractor-owned software, and handheld devices such as tablets and phones should not be included.

---

[6]GAO, *Federal Software Licenses: Better Management Needed to Achieve Significant Savings Government-Wide,* GAO-14-413 (Washington, D.C.: May 22, 2014).

For the second and third requirements, the plan's software licensing data collection instrument[7] contained key data fields necessary for the Office of the CIO to compare purchased licenses with installed licenses and assess the department's future needs. While data on license count are required, data on costs are to be entered only if readily available. Office of the CIO officials told us they expect the cost data they receive will be limited, but also stated that they are investigating how these data can be stored in a more centralized and automated fashion. Though cost information collected may be limited, these data could also inform the DOD CIO's future needs assessment for software licenses already in use (i.e., provide a basis for associated cost estimates). This forecasting of departmental requirements for software licensing purchases and other changes to inventory levels over the next 2 fiscal years may, among other things, allow DOD to take advantage of economies of scale while negotiating future licensing agreements.

Finally, for the fourth requirement, the plan outlined key analyses the DOD CIO and component CIOs expect to undertake once the department-wide inventory is complete, including the comparison of software licenses purchased with licenses installed; software licenses needs versus excess licenses; and assessments of alternative licensing options. Based on our work on leading practices in licensing management, the department's planned analyses could help achieve savings in license procurement, use,[8] and, to a limited degree, optimization—and thus generally meeting the purpose of the fourth requirement.

Among other things, these analyses could lead to savings through procuring volume discounts and/or moving toward enterprise-wide solutions; as well as disposing of excessive licenses.[9] Regarding license optimization, DOD's approach will enable it to match licenses installed

---

[7]The data collection instrument is a spreadsheet with key data fields (cells) to be filled in by the components for submission to the Office of the CIO for aggregate analysis. This spreadsheet also contains additional tabs with a data dictionary, among other things, to assist the components in determining the appropriate information to be provided.

[8]We defined license "use" as matching licenses deployed (installed) with licenses owned within an organization. Accordingly, this is also a form of license optimization.

[9]We reported in 2012 that most agencies including DOD only leveraged a fraction of their buying power. GAO, *Strategic Sourcing: Improved and Expanded Use Could Save Billions in Annual Procurement Costs*, GAO-12-919 (Washington, D.C.: Sep. 20, 2012).

and owned, but not match licenses owned with license usage (percentage of time a license is being actively used over a given period). This is because, according to Office of the CIO officials, obtaining data on license usage requires a level of software licensing management maturity that DOD has not yet achieved department-wide.

However, the official responsible for leading the inventory effort stated that another potential result of these analyses is that DOD may decide to increase automation or implement a more robust software license management system across the department. The Office of the CIO officials' assessment of the maturity of software license management department-wide is consistent with our work at DOD on our government-wide review. Further, as part of that report, we plan to make multiple recommendations which, if implemented appropriately, will better position DOD to determine license usage rates, among other things.

Table 1: Assessment of DOD's Plan for Developing an Inventory of Selected Software Licenses

Requirement	Addressed?
Identify and explain the software licenses selected, and provide a summary of the software licenses not selected.	●
Provide a comparison of purchased licenses with installed licenses.	●
Describe how the department will assess its needs for selected software licenses over the 2 fiscal years following plan issuance.	●
Describe how the department can achieve the greatest economies of scale and cost savings in the procurement, use, and optimization of selected software licenses.	●

Source: GAO analysis of DOD data. | GAO-14-625

Key:●=Addressed—DOD's plan provided evidence that addressed the requirement.

Concluding Observations

Because DOD procures numerous software license agreements annually, effectively managing them is critical to ensure that the department maximizes the value of these investments. DOD has developed a plan to help the department manage its licenses, and the plan clearly describes, among other statutory requirements, what software the inventory is to include. By identifying such information, DOD has laid the appropriate groundwork to analyze software license data.

DOD is currently implementing the plan, which will likely be the most challenging aspect of this effort. The DOD CIO's ability to effectively carry out its planned license efficiency analyses will depend largely on the completeness and accuracy of the information provided by the components.

Agency Comments

We are not making recommendations in this report. We provided a draft of this report to DOD for review and comment. In emailed comments, the Chief of the Office of the Inspector General, Office of Communications and Congressional Liaison, GAO Affairs Division stated that DOD reviewed the report and concurs.

We are sending copies of this report to the appropriate congressional committees, the Secretary of Defense, and other interested parties. In addition, the report is available at no charge on the GAO website at http://www.gao.gov.

Should you or your staffs have questions on matters discussed in this report, please contact me at (202) 512-4456 or ChaC@gao.gov. Contact points for our Offices of Congressional Relations and Public Affairs may be found on the last page of this report. GAO staff who made major contributions to this report are listed in appendix II.

Carol R. Cha
Director
Information Technology Acquisition Management Issues

List of Committees

The Honorable Carl Levin
Chairman
The Honorable James Inhofe
Ranking Member
Committee on Armed Services
United States Senate

The Honorable Richard J. Durbin
Chairman
The Honorable Thad Cochran
Ranking Member
Subcommittee on Defense
Committee on Appropriations
United States Senate

The Honorable Howard P. "Buck" McKeon
Chairman
The Honorable Adam Smith
Ranking Member
Committee on Armed Services
House of Representatives

The Honorable Rodney Frelinghuysen
Chairman
The Honorable Pete Visclosky
Ranking Member
Subcommittee on Defense
Committee on Appropriations
House of Representatives

Software Licenses: DOD's Plan to Collect Inventory Data Meets Statutory Requirements

Briefing for Staff Members of the

Committee on Armed Services, U.S. Senate;

Subcommittee on Defense, Committee on Appropriations, U.S. Senate;

Committee on Armed Services, House of Representatives;

and the

Subcommittee on Defense, Committee on Appropriations, House of Representatives

April 29, 2014

1

Contents

Introduction

Objective, Scope, and Methodology

Results in Brief

Background

Results

Concluding Observations

Agency Comments

2

Introduction

The Department of Defense (DOD) plans to spend at least $31 billion on information technology (IT) products and services in fiscal year 2014, including software licenses. Further, the department engages in hundreds of licensing agreements annually. Effective management of software licenses can help organizations avoid purchasing too many licenses that result in unused software and/or too few licenses that result in noncompliance with license terms, which can lead to additional fees.

To help DOD effectively manage its software licenses, Section 937 of the National Defense Authorization Act for Fiscal Year 2013[1] mandated the department to issue a plan for developing a DOD-wide inventory of selected[2] software licenses. DOD issued the plan on July 18, 2013. Further, the Senate report accompanying the act[3] mandated us to review and report by May 1, 2014, on whether DOD's plan addressed the following requirements specified in the act:

(1) Identify and explain the software licenses selected for inventory, and provide a summary of the software licenses not selected.

(2) Describe how the department will compare purchased licenses with installed[4] licenses.

---

[1]Pub. L. No. 112-239, § 937, 126 Stat. 1632, 1887-88 (Jan. 2, 2013). The act required DOD to issue the plan within 180 days of enactment.

[2]The act requires DOD's Chief Information Officer to select a subset of software licenses for inventory that will maximize the department's return on investment.

[3]S. Rep. No. 112-173, at 175 (2012).

[4]Software licenses deployed for use on a DOD owned or controlled computer.

3

Introduction

(3) Describe how the department will assess its needs for selected software licenses over the 2 fiscal years following plan issuance.

(4) Describe how the department can achieve the greatest economies of scale and cost savings in the procurement, use, and optimization of selected software licenses.

4

Objective, Scope, and Methodology

Our objective was to determine whether DOD's software license inventory plan met the following requirements specified in the act: (1) identify and explain the software licenses selected for inventory, and provide a summary of the software licenses not selected; (2) describe how the department will compare purchased licenses with installed licenses; (3) describe how the department will assess its needs for selected software licenses over the 2 fiscal years following plan issuance; (4) describe how the department can achieve the greatest economies of scale and cost savings in the procurement, use, and optimization of selected software licenses.

To accomplish our objective, we analyzed and compared DOD's plan to the four requirements above. Accordingly, we determined whether the plan satisfied or did not satisfy each requirement. In doing so, we also collected and analyzed key supporting materials, such as DOD's software license spend analysis, data collection instrument, and guidance provided to DOD components.

For requirement 1, we compared the spend analysis and meeting minutes from an IT research and advisory firm, among other things, to our work on federal software licensing[5] to determine the reasonableness of DOD's selection approach and results. For requirements 2 and 3, we evaluated the data collection instrument to determine whether key data fields needed to address the act were included. For requirement 4, we compared DOD's planned analysis approach against our key leading practice on software data analysis.

We also interviewed DOD officials from the Office of the Chief Information Officer (CIO) with knowledge of the plan.

---

[5]We are planning to issue our report on government-wide software licensing management in mid-May 2014. As part of this work, we identified leading licensing management practices, as well as major software publishers and products used government-wide.

5

Objective, Scope, and Methodology

We conducted this performance audit from March 2014 to April 2014 in accordance with generally accepted government auditing standards. Those standards require that we plan and perform the audit to obtain sufficient, appropriate evidence to provide a reasonable basis for our findings and conclusions based on our audit objectives. We believe that the evidence obtained provides a reasonable basis for our findings and conclusions based on our audit objective.

6

DOD's plan satisfied all four statutory requirements (see table 1). For example, for the first requirement, the plan contains detailed information on the scope of the inventory, including a list of over 900 software titles from publishers including Adobe, Microsoft, Oracle, and IBM. While the plan is sound, the implementation of the plan will be the most challenging part of this effort. The DOD CIO's ability to effectively carry out its planned cost savings analyses will largely depend on the completeness and accuracy of the information provided by the components.

Table 1: Assessment of DOD's Plan for Developing an Inventory of Selected Software Licenses

Requirement	Addressed?
Identify and explain the software licenses selected, and provide a summary of the software licenses not selected.	●
Provide a comparison of purchased licenses with installed licenses.	●
Describe how the department will assess its needs for selected software licenses over the 2 fiscal years following plan issuance.	●
Describe how the department can achieve the greatest economies of scale and cost savings in the procurement, use, and optimization of selected software licenses.	●

Key:
●=Addressed—DOD's plan provided evidence that addressed the requirement.
Source: GAO analysis of DOD data.

7

According to the Information Technology Infrastructure Library's *Guide to Software Asset Management*, software licenses are legal rights to use software in accordance with terms and conditions specified by the software copyright owner. Rights to use software are separate from the legal rights to the software itself, which are normally kept by the software manufacturer or other third party. Licenses may be bought and are normally required whenever externally acquired software is used, which will typically be when the software is installed on a computer (or when executed on a computer even if installed elsewhere such as on a server). They may also be defined in enterprise terms, such as number of workstations or employees, in which case a license is required for each qualifying unit or individual regardless of actual usage.[6]

More than 4 million desktop, laptop, and networked computers serve as essential tools for achieving the missions of federal agencies. The federal government engages in thousands of licensing agreements annually. We have ongoing work to evaluate the extent to which federal agencies, including DOD, are managing software licenses and expect to issue our report by mid-May 2014.

---

[6]Colin Rudd, *ITIL v.3 Guide to Software Asset Management* © *(2009), ISBN 9780113311064*. Reprinted with permission from ITIL. The guide is available at: http://www.axelos.com/Publications-Library/IT-Service-Management-ITIL/.

8

Background
DOD Software Licensing

The National Defense Authorization Act for Fiscal Year 2013 requires DOD's CIO, in consultation with the CIOs of the military departments and defense agencies, to issue a plan for the inventory of selected DOD software licenses. The act requires DOD's CIO to select software licenses that will maximize the return on investment in the inventory developed from the plan.

The act requires the plan to (1) identify and explain the software licenses selected for inventory, and provide a summary of the software licenses not selected; (2) describe how the department will compare purchased licenses with installed licenses; (3) describe how the department will assess its needs for selected software licenses over the 2 fiscal years following plan issuance; and (4) describe how the department can achieve the greatest economies of scale and cost savings in the procurement, use, and optimization of selected software licenses.

If DOD's CIO determines, through the inventory conducted pursuant to the plan, that the number of selected software licenses of the department and its components exceeds what is needed, the Secretary of DOD is to implement a plan to balance the number of selected software licenses with needs.

In response to the act, DOD's CIO issued a plan in July 2013. This plan provides guidance to the components on the scope, responsibilities, procedures, and schedule for completing an inventory of selected commercial off-the-shelf software licenses (through a data collection instrument). Office of the CIO officials stated this plan was distributed to approximately 30 components. According to the plan, component CIOs are expected to submit their completed data collection instruments by July 2014.

9

DOD CIO's software license inventory plan satisfied all four statutory requirements, as discussed below.

Requirement 1: Identify and explain the software licenses selected, and provide a summary of the software licenses not selected

The software license inventory plan identified detailed information on the scope of the inventory and described what software should be included. The list of licenses expected to be included in scope contained over 900 software titles from publishers including Adobe, Microsoft, Oracle, and IBM, all of which are commercial off-the-shelf[7] products. According to Office of the CIO officials, DOD's basis for the selected licenses was from a fiscal year 2011 software spend analysis,[8] consultation with subject matter experts from Gartner,[9] and discussions with component CIOs. These officials stated that, as a result of their assessment, they believed their list covers many of the licenses commonly held department-wide. Further, meeting minutes from the discussion with Gartner reflected that Gartner generally agreed with the list.

The selected publishers were also generally consistent with those that key agencies have also told us, as part of our work on federal software licensing, are being most widely used.

---

[7]According to the inventory plan, this software performs a specific operation or a series of operations and is sold in substantial quantities in the commercial market place.

[8]This analysis was completed by the Office of Defense Procurement and Acquisition Policy and showed the top software providers across DOD.

[9]Gartner is an IT research and advisory firm.

10

Results

The plan also summarized the software licenses not selected for inventory. More specifically, it outlined that some classified software, contractor-owned software, and handheld devices such as tablets and phones should not be included. The plan indicated that these licenses were not selected because they are not commercial off-the-shelf software products and/or widely used across the department.

11

Results

*Requirement 2: Describe how the department will compare purchased licenses with installed
licenses.*

The plan's software licensing data collection instrument[10] contained key data fields necessary for the
Office of the CIO to compare purchased licenses with installed licenses. The key data fields include
the count and cost of licenses (a) purchased since 2011, (b) maintained, and (c) installed on devices
or in a virtual environment.

While data on license count are required, costs are to be entered only if readily available. According
to an Office of CIO official, they determined through discussions with component CIOs that the cost
data are not maintained in a central repository,[11] but rather are stored within the components.
Further, the official stated that it would be manually intensive to map the costs of each license to its
source contract and contract amendments.

Data on the license counts will enable DOD to calculate whether it is purchasing too many or too few
licenses, while the cost data will enable it to effectively identify opportunities with the largest savings,
as well as estimate savings from resulting actions, such as reducing licenses. While Office of the CIO
officials told us they expect the cost data they receive will be limited, they also stated that they are
investigating how these data can be stored in a more centralized and automated fashion.

[10]The data collection instrument is a spreadsheet with key data fields (cells) to be filled in by the components for submission to the
Office of the CIO for aggregate analysis. This spreadsheet also contains additional tabs with a data dictionary, among other things, to
assist the components in determining the appropriate information to be provided.

[11]While the total value of a contract award is centrally listed in the Federal Procurement Data System-Next Generation, contract line-
item costs for individual licenses are not.

12

Requirement 3: Describe how the department will assess its needs for selected software licenses over the 2 fiscal years following plan issuance.

The plan's data collection instrument contained key data fields necessary for the Office of the CIO to assess the department's future software licensing needs. Key data fields include the number of licenses over fiscal years 2014 and 2015 needed to be (a) purchased, (b) upgraded, and/or (c) maintained.

According to an Office of the CIO official, although the licensing cost data to be collected in requirement 2 are expected to be limited, these data could also inform the DOD CIO's future needs assessment for software licenses already in use (i.e., provide a basis for associated cost estimates).

This forecasting of departmental requirements for software licensing purchases and other changes to inventory levels over the next 2 fiscal years may, among other things, allow DOD to take advantage of economies of scale while negotiating future licensing agreements.

13

Results

Requirement 4: Describe how the department can achieve the greatest economies of scale and cost savings in the procurement, use, and optimization of selected software licenses.

The plan outlined key analyses the DOD CIO and component CIOs expect to undertake once the department-wide inventory is complete, including (a) the comparison of software licenses purchased with licenses installed, (b) software licenses needs versus excess licenses, and (c) assessments of alternative licensing options.

Based on our work on leading practices in licensing management, the department's planned analyses could help achieve savings in license procurement, use,[12] and, to a limited degree, optimization—and thus generally meets the intent of requirement 4.

More specifically, regarding license procurement, evaluating alternative licensing options based on the extent to which the department has over- or under-purchased licenses could lead to savings through obtaining volume discounts and/or moving toward enterprise-wide solutions, among others. On savings derived from license use, the analyses (a) and (b) described above would support DOD's ability to match the licenses it owns with what has been installed, potentially leading to disposing of excessive licenses.

License optimization can be achieved through matching licenses installed and owned, but also through matching what is owned with license usage (percentage of time a license is being actively used over a given period). DOD's approach will enable it to address the former but not the latter.

---

[12]We defined license "use" as matching licenses deployed (installed) with licenses owned within an organization. Accordingly, this is also a form of license optimization.

14

Results

Office of the CIO officials stated that obtaining data on license usage requires a level of software licensing management maturity that they have not yet achieved department-wide. However, the official responsible for leading the inventory effort stated that another potential result of these analyses is that DOD may decide to increase automation or implement a more robust software license management system across the department.

The Office of the CIO officials' assessment of the maturity of software license management department-wide is consistent with our work at DOD on our government-wide review. Further, as part of that report, we plan to make multiple recommendations which, if implemented appropriately, will better position DOD to determine license usage rates, among other things.

15

Concluding Observations

Because DOD procures numerous software license agreements annually, effectively managing them is critical to ensure that the department maximizes the value of these investments. DOD has developed a plan to help the department manage its licenses, and the plan clearly describes, among other important statutory requirements, what software the inventory is to include. By identifying such information, DOD has laid the appropriate groundwork to analyze software license data.

DOD is currently implementing the plan, which will likely be the most challenging aspect of this effort. The DOD CIO's ability to effectively carry out its planned license efficiency analyses will depend largely on the completeness and accuracy of the information provided by the components.

16

Agency Comments

Officials from DOD's Office of the CIO provided oral comments on a draft of this briefing and stated that they generally agreed with our findings.

17

Appendix II: GAO Contact and Staff Acknowledgments

GAO Contact	Carol R. Cha, (202) 512-4456 or ChaC@gao.gov
Staff Acknowledgments	In addition to the contact name above, the following staff also made key contributions to this report: Eric Winter, Assistant Director; Eric Costello; Rebecca Eyler; Franklin Jackson; Scott Pettis; and Niti Tandon.